In Love Enclosed

IN LOVE ENCLOSED

More Daily Readings with
Julian of Norwich

Edited by
Robert Llewelyn

Introduced by Michael McLean
Translated by Sheila Upjohn
Illustrated by Irene Ogden

Darton, Longman and Todd
London

First published in 1985 by
Darton, Longman and Todd Ltd
89 Lillie Road, London SW6 1UD

© 1985 The Julian Shrine

ISBN 0 232 51638 3

British Library Cataloguing in Publication Data

Llewelyn, Robert
  In love enclosed: more daily readings with
Julian of Norwich.
  1. Devotional calendars
  I. Title
  242′.2   BV4810

  ISBN 0–232–51638–3

All royalties earned by the sale
of this book are being given to
The Julian Shrine, c/o All Hallows
Rouen Road, Norwich

Phototypeset by
Input Typesetting Ltd, London SW19 8DR
Printed and bound in Great Britain by
Anchor Brendon Ltd, Tiptree, Essex

Contents

Editor's Preface

Enfolded in Love, the first book in this series of devotional readings, was compiled by four members of the Julian Shrine who, in 1980, preferred to remain anonymous. They are now offering further selections from Julian's *Revelations of Divine Love* under the companion title *In Love Enclosed*.

The earlier volume ranged over the full extent of the *Revelations* and was necessarily fragmentary in character. It was pre-eminently a devotional manual. The aim of the present work is to provide the theological substance of Julian's thought and at the same time to present it in a form suitable for devotional use. The devotional richness of Julian's writings springs from the theological perception and integrity which inspires them. Perhaps this book may best be seen as a halfway house between *Enfolded in Love* and the complete work. Here we have consecutive readings covering one or more complete chapters a step at a time, and there are many people who may welcome this gradual approach. Julian's book, when tackled in full, may well be found somewhat daunting for the general reader.

In this approach we are, however, up against a difficulty. In a book limited like others in this series to sixty readings, it is only possible to cover about one half of Julian's complete work. We hope, therefore, to produce a further volume at some later stage, drawing in the same way on the second half of the *Revelations*.

Michael McLean, whose work as Rector of St Julian's has done so much to encourage the developing work of the Shrine, and who assisted in the editing of *Enfolded in Love*, has in his introduction outlined the main aspects of Julian's thought in the pages which follow. Sheila Upjohn has again given us the benefit of her clear and fresh translation, and Irene Ogden's attractive drawings are to be found once more on the cover and inside pages. I would like to express my gratitude for their help here as in the earlier book.

ROBERT LLEWELYN
The Julian Shrine,
c/o All Hallows,
Rouen Road,
Norwich.

Introduction

In 1972 the Dean of Norwich gathered a group of people to plan how the 600th anniversary of the Shewings to Lady Julian might be celebrated the following year. At one committee meeting it was suggested that what was needed to make Julian's thought accessible to a wide public was a selection of passages from her book *Revelations of Divine Love*. It was not until 1980, however, at the initiative of Father Robert Llewelyn, by then Chaplain at the Shrine where Julian had lived, that this idea came to fruition. *Enfolded in Love* rapidly became a best-seller, introducing thousands of people to 'one of the most wonderful of Christian voices'. This present volume takes the selection a stage further.

In twelve years Julian's popularity has grown enormously. A number of editions of her book have been published, and it has been translated into several foreign languages; some major critical works have appeared, and all over the world scholarly and devotional studies have been written. Julian herself has been included in the new Church of England Calendar, and for some people she has become virtually their 'patron saint'. In America a religious Order has been founded bearing her name, and in England well over a hundred 'Julian Groups' encourage the practice of contemplative prayer. Thousands of pilgrims visit her shrine in Norwich each year, many linking themselves with the work there by becoming 'Friends of St Julian's'.

How is it that the thought of an obscure Norfolk woman, almost forgotten for 600 years, has become so influential? What is it about the visions of a fourteenth-century recluse – a style of life which seems so alien to our contemporaries – which speaks so relevantly to the condition of twentieth-century men and women?

A WOMAN OF COURAGE

The answer to these questions may well lie in the similarities between her day and ours.

Hers was an age of aggression – the Hundred Years War abroad, and political unrest at home; so perhaps is ours. Hers was an age of fear and social distress – the Black Death ravaging the population, and questionings of existing structures; so perhaps is ours. Hers was an age when the Church was in some disarray – religious rivalries, rival popes, and doctrinal controversy; so perhaps is ours. Hers was an age when new philosophical and theological ideas were sweeping Europe, culminating a little later in the Reformation; so perhaps is ours. Both the fourteenth century and the twentieth are marked by excitement, mobility, disturbance.

Julian, enclosed in her cell yet free in spirit, at once reflects and challenges her day. Certainly there is no single direct reference in her book to contemporary events, but, it can be claimed, they lie behind the 'givenness' of her revelations. Her stability, her patience and assurance are matched by an adventurous, brave and inquiring spirit. She is unafraid to push at the boundaries of doctrinal orthodoxy, yet she is the submissive daughter of the Church. Facing realistically the paradoxes and sufferings of the Christian life, she is yet grounded in that peace which comes from total belief in and acceptance of the love of God. 'He did not say "you shall not be afflicted, you shall not be tempest-tossed," ' she writes, 'but he did say "you shall not be overcome".'[1]

This blessed assurance stemmed from the visions she was granted by God on 8 May 1373. After a week's illness involving great physical and spiritual distress, and which it was thought could culminate only in death, she received while she gazed at a crucifix sixteen understandings of the amazing love of God. For many years before, she had patiently sought his will; for twenty years and more afterwards she patiently teased out the significances of these 'shewings' by prayer and profound thought. In a sense, too, she has patiently waited 600 years for a generation receptive to her message, for, until this century, her book has been largely unknown. And it is not insignificant that 'patience' and 'suffering' have the same linguistic root, for Julian knows a great deal about the pain of life and the problem of evil.

Her theology may well start, as has been said, 'from the sun, not the clouds', but she has an acute sense of sin. 'The shadows are deep because the light is so bright.' Julian is a realist about the human condition, with no hint of the airy-fairy ecstatic mystic about her. Mystic she may be, but

1 See p. 39 of *Enfolded in Love*, or ch. 68 of *Revelations of Divine Love*.

she is utterly down-to-earth because her heart and mind are so utterly in heaven.

It is probably these qualities which have made Julian's thought so helpful and relevant to twentieth-century men and women. In a Church and society which have lamentably divorced head and heart so often – over-cerebral and materialistic on the one hand, and sensation-seeking and woolly-minded on the other – Julian's realization that God is concerned with the whole of man – body, mind, and spirit – and her insistence on the fundamental unity of man's being with the all-embracing love of God, have much to teach us today.

A selection such as this book contains, taken from only the first half of the *Revelations*, cannot cover all her thought. But most of her leading ideas are at least foreshadowed in these pages, and it may be useful to point to a few of them in the hope that readers will be encouraged to explore the full text of her book.

THE CENTRAL VISION

First, like authentic mystics of all religious traditions, she has an overwhelming sense of the centrality of God. God is 'our Maker and Keeper, our everlasting love, our joy, our bliss'.[1] He 'is all that is good . . . and God has made all that is made.'[2]. So the perfect response of man is to seek that good: 'This seeking with faith, hope and love pleases our Lord, and the finding pleases the soul and fills it full of joy.'[3] It is a journey which has

1   P. 7.   2   P. 9.   3   P. 12.

its end in the vision of God, yet even here and now we have glimpses of his glory: 'I saw him and I sought him, and I had him and I lacked him.'[1]

The vision of God, both here and hereafter, is possible because God is the ground of all that exists – its maker, sustainer, and redeemer. Nothing is outside his constant creative will. In her famous vision of a little thing 'the size of a hazel-nut in the palm of my hand',[2] or in the 'shewing' of God 'in a point',[3] she is led to understand God's loving concern for all he has made. And this leads her to the realization that God loves our fallen human nature just as much as our redeemed humanity. In fact there is no division between the two, for Christ in assuming the former at the incarnation can raise it to the latter by the power of his resurrection life. God wills that what Julian calls our 'sensuality' should be raised to the same glory as our inner being or 'substance' as she calls it. 'Every kind of "nature" that he has caused to flow out of himself to fulfil his purpose will be brought back and restored to him.'[4] So it is that her most famous aphorism, 'all shall be well', is not an optimism grounded in humanist hope, but a divinely-given certainty that what God loves – and he loves all that is – he will take to himself. An age which tends to separate

1 P. 10.
2 See p. 3 of *Enfolded in Love*, or ch. 5 of *Revelations of Divine Love*.
3 See p. 11 of *Enfolded in Love*, or ch. 11 of *Revelations of Divine Love*.
4 See ch. 62 of *Revelations of Divine Love*.

the 'spiritual' and the 'material' needs to hear this, and certainly it challenges our attitude towards the creation, especially our own humanity. For Julian, to be fully human is to be in God, and the supernatural is what is most truly natural.

THE COMPASSIONATE GOD

Julian arrives at this understanding because she is so vitally aware of the incredible totality of God's love. This love is all-enfolding, warm and tender. As Julian gazed at the image of the Crucified she saw that in the passion of the Son (the supreme act of divine love) there is a revealing of the essential compassion of the Father. Certainly she sometimes writes of the inexpressible glory and majesty of God, his utter transcendence, but generally she is at pains to underline this compassion, his intimate yearning love for each soul. She piles image upon image – most notably, perhaps, in her image of Christ's motherhood – in the attempt to describe this generous gentle love. God is the courteous Lord who offers man a princely friendship, and wants us to be joined to him in joyful love.

Such an understanding has two consequences.

First, it makes any belief in a wrathful God quite impossible. There can be no anger in him. What we seem to experience as anger, what we call anger, is in fact completely in ourselves, and is simply a name to express the sensation caused in a sinner by the fire of God's love. 'Anger is no more than a perversity and striving against peace and love. And it is caused either by lack of strength, or lack of wisdom, or lack of goodness. This lack is not found in God, but in us.'[1]

The second consequence is that it leads us to understand that we must love ourselves. This is no new idea; Jesus himself taught it, following the old Law, 'thou shalt love thy neighbour as thyself'. But it is a command too frequently neglected. 'It is his will that we should be like him in wholeness of endless love towards ourselves and our fellow-Christians. And just as he does not stop loving us because of our sin, so he wills that we should not stop loving ourselves or our fellow-Christians.'[2] It is probable that more harm has been caused to people's healthy development by self-hatred than by immoderate self-love. Julian teaches us to love the soul as God loves it. That all-too-common distortion of Christianity which emphasizes self-abnegation to the point of despising or rejecting self, and the frequently-found inability to forgive self, are corrected by Julian's true humanity.

Yet, as has already been pointed out, Julian is a realist. She knows, both from her personal history and the revelation of the price Christ paid on the cross, the bitter reality of sin and pain. But God shows her that his love is so great that by his mercy all the falls and suffering which human beings endure are somehow taken up into his divine purpose, and are used by him to bring us to perfection. This is a message of great joy and hope to those of us who find ourselves unlovable,

1 P. 53.   2 P. 47.

or who think our lives are depressingly fallible and futile.

A generation which has learnt from psychology the dangers inherent in guilt-feelings and tries to avoid them by writing off the concepts of sin and moral responsibility, needs to hear Julian. Her approach is saner. She fully recognizes the horror of sin (though in her view it has no being in itself), but she also knows that it is 'behovely',[1] for it will bring us nearer to God if we will let it. She is concerned not with guilt-feelings but with penitence. And penitence is the recognition of God's loving mercy, and total reliance upon it. 'Our failing is fearful, our falling is full of shame . . . but the sweet eye of pity and love never looks away from us, nor does the working of mercy ever cease.'[2] This is a great comfort to those so often oppressed by their constant falls and sin.

MAN'S GLORIOUS HOPE

All these things and more came to Lady Julian in the contemplation of God's love focused in the Passion of Christ. She was shown there the wonderful purposes of God. She writes them down so that we might share her confidence and hope. It is a message which speaks vividly to an often frightened and bewildered generation. 'When we can find no rest, he works continually to bring us to peace that shall never end . . . and our Lord takes our strivings and sends them up to heaven where they are made more delectable than heart can think, or tongue can tell . . . So

1   P. 29.   2   P. 54.

God is our sure rock, and he shall be our whole joy, and make us changeless as he is, when we reach heaven.'[1]

This is the blessed assurance which speaks across 600 years. It is an assurance Julian wishes to share with us, her fellow-pilgrims, as we journey towards that glory which God's love offers to us all. Many thousands of people have found in the *Revelations* this great hope, and while Julian bids us forget her, we may be sure she rejoices that it is so.

MICHAEL MCLEAN

1 P. 59.

Three Gifts from God

These revelations were to a plain, unlettered woman in the year of our Lord 1373, on the eighth day of May.

This woman had asked for three gifts from God. The first was to understand his Passion; the second was to have an illness in her youth when she was thirty years old; the third was to have, by God's grace, three wounds.

As to the first, I thought I already knew something of Christ's Passion, but I wanted to know even more by God's grace. I wished I had been there with Mary Magdalene and those others who were Christ's friends.

And so I asked for an actual sight – through which I should have more understanding of the compassion of our Lady and of all his friends who saw his agony and pain at that time. I wanted to be one of them and suffer with him.

I asked for no other sight or showing from God until the time came for my soul to leave my body.

The reason for this petition was that afterwards I might have better understanding of the Passion of Christ.

The Second Petition

The second petition came to my mind as I repented of sin.

I asked for an illness so close to death that I might in that illness receive the last rites of the Church; that I myself should believe I was dying – and so should everyone around me. For I wanted to loose my hold on earthly life.

In this illness I asked to have all the bodily and spiritual pain I should have if I were actually dying, with all the terrors and torments of devils, except only this – that my soul should not leave my body.

I asked this so that I might be cleansed by the mercy of God, and afterwards live more to his glory because of that illness – and also to ease my death when it came, because I should be glad to go to God.

These two petitions, for the Passion and the illness, I asked with a condition, saying this: 'Lord, you know what I desire, but I desire it only if it is your will that I should have it. If it is not your will, good Lord, do not be displeased, for my will is to do your will.'

The Third Petition

As for the third petition, by God's grace and the teaching of Holy Church, I was filled with an overwhelming desire to receive three wounds in this life.

That is to say, the wound of true repentance, the wound of suffering as Christ suffered, and the wound of seeking God with all my strength. I made this petition without any condition.

The other two desires passed from my mind and the third was with me continually.

Julian Receives the Last Rites

And when I was thirty-and-a-half years old, God sent me an illness which held me three days and three nights. On the fourth night I received all the rites of Holy Church and did not think to live until day. And after this I lingered on two days and two nights. And on the third night I often thought I was dying, and so did those who were with me.

And, young as I was, I thought it was sad to die: not because of anything on earth I wanted to live for, and not because of any pain I was afraid of – for I trusted God's mercy – but because if I had lived I should have been able to love God better and for longer, so that I should know God better and love him more in the joy of heaven.

For I thought that the time I had lived here on earth was too small and too short to deserve that endless joy – it seemed like nothing.

And so I thought: 'Good Lord, if I live no longer, may it be to your glory!'

And I understood in my mind and my body that I should die. And I assented to it with my heart and will, that God's will should be my will.

Julian Looks upon the Cross

And so I lasted until day, and by then my body was dead from the waist down, as I felt. Then I asked to be propped upright, leaning on others, so I should have more freedom in my heart to be at God's command and to think on God for as long as my life should last.

My priest was sent for to be at my end, and by the time he came, my eyes were set and I could not speak. He held the cross before me and said: 'I have brought you the likeness of your Maker and Saviour. Look upon it, and draw comfort from it.'

I thought I was doing right, for my eyes were turned upwards towards heaven where I trusted to go by the mercy of God. Nevertheless, I told myself to turn my eyes to the cross if I could, and I did so, even though I had thought that I could look nowhere except upwards.

After this, my sight began to fail and it was all dark around me in the room as if it were night – except for the cross. I saw it glow with light and I did not know how. Everything, except the cross, was hideous to me as if it were possessed by devils.

Julian Asks for the Second Wound

After this, the upper part of my body began to die, so completely that I had hardly any feeling and could scarcely breathe. And then I truly thought I was dying. At this moment, suddenly all my pain was taken from me and I was as well, particularly in the upper part of my body, as ever I was before. I marvelled at this sudden change, for I thought it was a special work of God and not of nature. And yet by feeling this ease I did not think to live, nor was this ease a comfort to me, for I thought I would rather be delivered from the world.

Then suddenly it came to my mind that I should ask for the second wound, by our Lord's gracious gift – that my body might be used to give me knowledge and understanding of his blessed Passion. For I willed that his pains should be my pains – by compassion and then by longing for God.

In all this I never asked for an actual sight or showing from God, but simply to suffer with him – as a loving soul might want to share with our Lord Jesus, who for love became a mortal man. And for this I asked to suffer with him.

The First Showing

At this, suddenly I saw the red blood trickle down from under the crown of thorns, hot and fresh and flooding out as it did at the time of his Passion when the crown of thorns was pressed into his blessed head – he who was both God and man and who suffered for me.

And in this same Showing, suddenly the Trinity filled my heart full of joy. And I understood that this is how it will be in heaven without end, for those who come here.

For the Trinity is God, and God is the Trinity. The Trinity is our Maker and Keeper. The Trinity is our everlasting love, our joy and our bliss, through our Lord Jesus Christ.

And this was shown in the first revelation and in them all. For when Jesus appears, the blessed Trinity is understood, as I see it.

And I said: 'Blessed be God!' I said this with reverence in my heart and with a loud voice. And I was astounded at the wonder of it, that he, who is so high and holy, will be so homely with a sinful soul living in frail flesh.

Embracing God's Love

I said to those who were near me: 'Today is Judgement Day for me.' I said this because I thought I was going to die, and on the day a man dies he is judged as he shall be judged for ever, as I see it. I said this because I wanted them to love God better, and to help them to amend their short lives by this example.

All this time I thought I was going to die and it was a wonder to me, and a sort of sorrow, for I thought this Showing was meant for those who were going to live.

And what I say from myself I say as from all my fellow-Christians, for I am taught by God, through this holy showing, that this is his meaning.

Therefore I pray you all, for God's sake, and tell you for your own good, that you do not let your eye dwell on the humble woman this was shown to, but let your sight go beyond and wisely, humbly and mightily behold God who, by his courteous love and endless goodness, wishes it to be widely known to comfort us all.

For it is God's will that you should embrace his love with great joy and gladness, as Jesus has shown it to you, one and all.

Bound Together in Love

Because of this showing, I am not good: I am only good if I love God better. If you love God better than I do, you are that much better than I am. I do not say this to those who are wise, for they know it well, but I say it to you who are simple to cheer and comfort you – for we all need comfort.

For truly it was not shown to me that God loved me better than he loves the humblest soul that is in grace, for I am sure there are many who never had sign or showing, except for the ordinary teaching of Holy Church, who love God better than I do. For if I look at myself alone, I am nothing. But when I think of myself and my fellow-Christians joined together by love, I have hope. For in our shared love lies the salvation of all who shall be saved.

For God is all that is good, as I see it, and God has made all that is made; and he who embraces all his fellow-Christians in love for God's sake, loves all that is made.

For in mankind that shall be saved everything is brought together – that is to say, all that is made and the Maker of all. And I hope, by the grace of God, he who understands this shall be truly taught and greatly comforted, if he has need of comfort.

The Second Showing

 And after this, in my outward sight, I saw a part of his Passion in Christ's face on the cross, which was in front of me, and which I looked at continually. I saw how he was scorned and spat upon and sullied and beaten – and many long-drawn agonies (more than I can tell you), and how the colour of his face often changed.

I saw this with my outward sight, dimly and darkly, and I asked for better light, so as to see more clearly. And I was answered in my mind: 'If God wills to show you more, he will be your light. You have need of none but him.' For I saw him while I sought him.

Here we are so blind and so foolish that we never look for God until he in his goodness shows himself to us. When we see something of him, through his grace, then we are guided by the same grace to seek him with great longing and to see him more joyfully.

And so I saw him and I sought him, and I had him and I lacked him. And this is and should be our usual way, as I see it.

God Is Present Everywhere

At one time my mind was led down to the bottom of the sea, and there I saw hills and green valleys looking as if they were covered with moss and seaweed and sand.

Then I understood this: that if a man or woman were under the wide waters, as long as he could still see God (and God is with us always), he should be safe in body and soul and take no harm. And over and above this, he would have more cheer and comfort than all the world can tell.

For he wills that we believe we can see him all the time continually, even though it seems to us we see him very little. When we believe this, he helps us all the time to get grace. For his will is to be seen and to be sought, his will is to be waited for and trusted.

And this Showing was to teach me that when the soul continually seeks God, it pleases him greatly. For the soul can do no more than seek, suffer and trust, and this is the work of the Holy Spirit in the soul. And the clearness in finding him comes by his special grace, when it is his will.

This seeking with faith, hope and love pleases our Lord, and the finding pleases the soul and fills it full of joy.

And so I was taught in my mind that seeking is as good as seeing during the time he lets the soul labour. It is God's will that we seek after him to see him, so that he can show himself to us by his special grace, when it is his will.

And he himself shall teach a soul how it may come to have a sight of him. And this is most glory to him and profit to you, and the richest way to receive meekness and virtue by the guidance of the Holy Ghost. For a soul that entirely clings to him with true trust, either of seeking or seeing, brings the highest worship it can to him, as I see it.

Three Qualities in Our Seeking

There are two works that can be seen in this showing; one is seeking, the other is seeing.

The seeking is commonplace – that is, every soul can undertake it by his grace, and ought to do so by the direction and teaching of Holy Church.

It is God's will that we have three things in our seeking.

The first is that we seek willingly and actively, without sloth, as we can through his grace, gladly and happily, without foolish gladness and empty sorrow.

The second is that we wait on him steadfastly for love, not grumbling and striving against him, until our life's end – for it lasts so short a time.

The third is that we trust him completely with certainty of faith, because this is his will.

We know he will come suddenly and joyfully to all who love him. For his way is secret, his way is to be seen, his coming shall be right sudden, and his will is to be trusted – for he is gracious and homely. Blessed may he be!

The Fourth Showing

And after this, as I looked, I saw the body bleeding freely from the weals made by the scourging. The fair skin was driven deep into the tender flesh by the harsh striking all over the sweet body.

The warm blood ran out so freely that there was neither skin nor wound to be seen but, as it were, all blood. And when the blood came to the place where it should have begun to drip down, it vanished. Even so, the bleeding continued for a long time, so it could be seen and understood. And the bleeding, as I saw it, was so plentiful that I thought that if it had been real and substantial then it would have soaked the bed with blood and flowed all round about it.

And then it came into my mind that God has made many waters in earth for our use and our comfort, because of his dear love for us. But yet it pleases him better that we should simply and humbly take his blessed blood to wash away our sins.

For there is no liquid made that he likes so much to give us. For it is as plentiful as it is precious, and it is all this by virtue of his blessed Godhead. It comes naturally to us and blessedly flows over us by virtue of his precious love. The most dear blood of our Lord Jesus Christ is as precious as it is plentiful. Look and see!

The Amplitude of God's Saving Love

The precious plenty of his dear blood went down into hell and broke its bonds and delivered all those who were there who belonged to the court of heaven.

The precious plenty of his dear blood overflows all the earth and waits to wash away the sin of all people who are of good will.

The precious plenty of his dear blood went up to heaven to the blessed body of our Lord Jesus Christ and is there within him, bleeding and praying for us to the Father – and is and shall be for as long as it is needed.

And evermore it flows through all the heavens, rejoicing in the salvation of mankind, those who are there and those who shall be, making up the number of those who shall be saved.

The Fifth Showing

And after this, before God spoke any word, he allowed me to look upon him for a while. And all that I had seen and all the meaning of it was there, as far as the simplicity of my soul could understand it. Then he, without voice or opening his lips, formed these words in my soul: 'By this is the fiend overcome.' Our Lord said these words meaning his blessed Passion, which he showed before.

In this our Lord showed that it is his Passion that is the fiend's undoing. God showed that the fiend has the same malice now as he had before the incarnation. And as hard as he works, so he continually sees that all the souls of salvation escape him, gloriously, by the virtue of Christ's Passion. And this is his sorrow, and he is put down, full of evil.

For all that God allows him to do turns to joy to us, but it turns to shame and woe to him. And he has as much pain when God gives him leave to work as when he is idle. And this is because he can never do as much evil as he would like, for his power is all taken into God's hands.

The Devil Is Scorned

But in God there can be no anger, as I see it. For our good Lord always has in his mind his own goodness and the rewarding of all who shall be saved. He sets his might and his right in the path of the Evil One who, for wickedness and malice, busies himself to plot and work against God's will. Also, I saw our Lord scorn the devil's malice and expose his lack of power, and he wills that we should do so, too.

Because I saw this sight I laughed aloud and made those who were round me laugh too, and their laughing rejoiced my heart. I wanted all my fellow-Christians to see what I saw, so they would all laugh with me.

But I did not see Christ laugh, although I understood that we may laugh aloud in comforting ourselves and rejoicing in God because the devil is overcome.

I thought of Judgement Day and of all those who shall be saved, whose happiness he greatly envies. For at that day he shall see that all the grief and trouble he has brought upon them shall be turned into even greater joy for them, without end, and all the pain and tribulation he wished upon them shall go with him to hell, without end also.

The Sixth Showing

God showed three kinds of joy that every soul who has served God willingly on earth shall have in heaven. The first is the wonderful thanks of our Lord God, which shall be his as soon as he is delivered from this world's pain. This thanks is so great and glorious that he will think it fills him to the brim, even if there were no more to come. For I thought that all the toil and trouble that all mortal men together could suffer would not be enough to deserve the glorious thanks that just one man shall have who has served God willingly.

The second kind of joy is that this glorious giving of thanks shall be seen by all the blessed souls that are in heaven. For God makes a man's service to him known to all the heavenly host. And then an example of this was shown me: if a king thanks his servants, it is great praise to them; but if he makes it known throughout his kingdom, then the glory is that much greater.

The third kind of joy is this: that the freshness and delight of that moment shall last for ever.

The Reward of Willing Service

 And I saw this simply and sweetly shown: that every man's age shall be known in heaven, and he shall be rewarded for his willing service and for the length of time he has given it. And particularly those who freely and willingly offer their youth to God shall be specially rewarded and wonderfully thanked.

For I saw that no matter when or for how long a man or woman is truly turned to God, even for one day's service given with his whole will, he shall have all three kinds of joy without end.

And the more a living soul sees this graciousness of God, the more he wants to serve him all the days of his life.

The Seventh Showing

And after this, he put a most high inward happiness in my soul. I was filled full of endless certainty and it was sustained so strongly that it left no room for doubts and fears. This feeling was so happy and so holy and put me in such peace and rest that there was nothing on earth that had the power to make me sad. This lasted only a while, and then my mood was changed and I was left on my own in sadness and weariness of life. I loathed myself so much that I could hardly bear to live. There was nothing to comfort me or give me any ease except for faith, hope and love. And although I knew them to be true, they gave me little joy.

And soon after this, our blessed Lord gave me again that comfort and rest of soul so blissful and mighty in its sureness and delight that no fear, no sorrow and no bodily pain that I might suffer could have taken away my peace. And then the sadness once more overcame my mind, and then the joy and gladness, and now the one, and now the other – I suppose about twenty times.

And in the time of joy I might have said with St Paul: 'Nothing shall separate me from the love of Christ.' And in the sadness I might have said with St Peter: 'Lord, save me, for I perish.'

The Meaning of the Revelation

This vision was shown me, as I understand it, because it is necessary to some souls to feel in this way – sometimes to know comfort, and sometimes to fail and be left on their own. God wants us to know that he keeps us safe through good and ill.

For his soul's sake a man is sometimes left on his own, but his sin is not always the cause. For during this time I did not sin, so why should I have been forsaken, and so suddenly? Also, I did nothing to deserve this feeling of bliss.

But our Lord freely gives what it is his will to give, and sometimes lets us suffer woe – and both are part of one love. For bliss is lasting and pain is passing and shall come to nothing for those that shall be saved.

And therefore it is not God's will that we should linger over pain, but that we should pass quickly through it to joy without end.

The Eighth Showing

That day when our blessed Lord and Saviour died upon the cross there was a dry, frosty wind that was bitter cold, as I saw it. And when all the precious blood that could, had bled out of his dear body, yet there was still moisture in his dear flesh, as I was shown. Loss of blood, and pain, dried it from within; wind and cold dried it from without; and both met together in Christ's body. And these four, two within and two without, dried Christ's flesh in the process of time.

And although the pain of it was sharp and bitter, it was also long-drawn-out, as I saw it, and agonizingly dried out all the living essence of Christ's flesh. So I saw his dear flesh die, part by part, as it seemed, drying out with dreadful pain. And as long as there was any living essence in Christ's flesh, so long was he in agony.

The pain was so long-drawn-out that it seemed to me as if he had been seven nights dead, dying, at the point of death, enduring those last pains. When I say it was as if he had been dead a week, I mean that his dear body was so discoloured, so dried-out, so withered, so deathlike and so pitiful that he might have been seven nights dead, and dying, every one. And I thought that the dying of his flesh was the last and most painful part of his Passion.

The Sharing of the Passion

This showing of Christ's pain filled me full of pain, for though I knew well enough he suffered only once, yet it was his will to show me and fill my mind with it, as I had often asked before. And in all this time of Christ's pain, I felt only his pain and no pain of my own besides.

Then I thought: 'I little knew what pain it was I asked for', and like a fool regretted it, thinking that if I had known what it would be like, I should not have prayed to suffer it. For I thought this pain was worse than death itself, my pain. I thought: 'Is any pain like this?' and I was answered in my mind: 'Hell is a different pain, for then there is despair. But of all the pains that lead to salvation, this is the worst pain – to see your love suffer.'

How could any pain be worse to me than to see him suffer who is my whole life, my whole bliss and my whole joy? Then I knew truly that I loved Christ so much more than myself that there could be no pain like the grief I had, to see him suffer.

The Love of Our Lady Saint Mary

Here I saw part of the love and suffering of our Lady Saint Mary, for she and Christ were so joined in love that the greatness of his love caused the greatness of her grief. And so in this I saw the instinctive love, led on by grace, that all creation has for him.

This natural love was shown most of all by his dear mother and surpassed all others, for as she loved him more than all the rest, by so much was her pain beyond all theirs.

For the higher, the greater and the sweeter the love is, so the greater grief it is to those who love, to see their loved one suffer.

And all his disciples and all those at that time who truly loved him suffered more then than if they had died themselves. For I am sure, by what I felt myself, that the least of them loved him so much more than themselves that it goes beyond all that I can say.

Here I saw a great communion between Christ and ourselves as I see it, for when he was in pain, we were in pain. And all creation capable of feeling pain suffered with him – that is to say, all creatures that God has made to serve us.

You Are My Heaven

And then I wanted to look away from the cross, and I dared not. For I knew well that while I looked at the cross I was safe and sure. I did not want to put my soul in peril, for there was no safety from the terrors of devils, except for the cross.

Then I heard a word in my ear that kindly said to me: 'Look up to heaven to his Father.'

Then I saw clearly by faith that there was nothing between the cross and heaven that could have done me any harm. Either I had to look up or to answer.

I answered inwardly with all my soul's strength and said: 'No, I cannot, for you are my heaven.' This I said because I did not want to look away – for I had rather have borne that pain until the Day of Judgement than come to heaven any other way than through him. For I knew well that he who bound me so fast could unbind me when he chose.

So I was taught to choose Jesus for my heaven, though I saw him only in pain at that time. I wanted no other heaven than Jesus, who shall be my joy when I come there.

He Suffered for Us

The deepest truth of the Passion is to know and understand who he was that suffered. And in this he allowed me to understand a part of the height and nobleness of the glorious Godhead, and also the worth and tenderness of the blessed body with which it is made one, and also the loathing our nature has for pain.

For as much as he was pure and loving, even so much was he strong and able to suffer – for it was the sin of every man that shall be saved which he suffered for. And he saw the sorrow and desolation of every one of us, and grieved over it for love because he shared our nature. For as greatly as our Lady grieved over his pain, he grieved for her grief just as much – and more – because the manhood he bore was of even greater worth.

For as long as he was capable of suffering, he suffered and sorrowed for us. And now that he is risen and can feel pain no more, yet still he suffers with us.

And I, seeing all this through his grace, saw that the love he has for our soul is so strong that he sought our soul with great longing, and willingly suffered for it and paid for it in full.

For a soul that looks on these things shall see, when it is touched by grace, that the pains of Christ's Passion go beyond all other pain and, true to tell, that these same pains shall be turned into endless joys through Christ's Passion.

We Shall Be Wholly Blessed

And I looked for the moment of his death with all my strength and thought to have seen his body quite lifeless, but I did not see him so. And just at the same moment, it seemed, that I thought that life could last no longer and the sight of his end must be shown, suddenly as I looked at that same cross, his expression changed to joy.

The change in his blessed mood changed mine, and I was as glad and as merry as can be. Then our Lord brought this gladly into my mind: 'Where is any part of your pain and grief now?' And I was overjoyed.

I understood that our Lord means that in this life we are on his cross with him in our pain and sorrow and our dying, and that if, of our own free will, we stay on that cross, with his help and grace, until the last moment, suddenly his expression will change and we shall be with him in heaven. Between the one and the other there shall be no lapse of time, but at once everything shall be changed to joy.

And this is what he meant when he said to me: 'Where is any part of your pain and grief now?' And we shall be wholly blessed. And here I saw truly that, if he showed us his joyful expression now, there is no pain on earth or in any other place that could grieve us – but everything should fill us with joy and gladness.

The Eleventh Showing

And with this same look of joy and happiness, our good Lord looked down to his right and made me remember where our Lady stood at the time of his Passion. And he said: 'Would you like to see her?'

And in these sweet words it was as if he said: 'I know full well that you would like to see my blessed mother, for she is the greatest delight, after myself, that I could show you – the one dearest to me and the one who gives me highest praise. She is most worth seeing of all that I have made.'

And because of the high and wonderful love he had specially for this sweet maiden, his blessed mother, our Lady Saint Mary, he showed her greatly rejoicing, as if he used words that said: 'Would you like to see how I love her, so that you can rejoice with me in the love I have for her, and she for me?'

And, so that we should understand even better, our Lord speaks to all mankind who shall be saved as if they were all just one person – as though he said: 'Can you see in her how you yourself are loved? It was for love of you that I made her so high, so noble and so good. And this brings me great joy, and I want it to bring you joy, too.'

The Thirteenth Showing

After this, the Lord brought into my mind the longing I had for him before, and I saw that nothing stood in my way but sin, and I saw this was the same for all of us. And it seemed to me that, if sin had not been, we should all have been clean and like our Lord, the way he made us. And so, in my folly, before this time I had often wondered why, by the great foreseeing wisdom of God, the beginning of sin was not prevented, for then, I thought, all should have been well.

I should have left off this worrying; nevertheless, I mourned and sorrowed over it without reason or discretion. But Jesus, who in the showing told me all that I needed, answered by this word and said: 'Sin is behovely – it had to be – but all shall be well, and all shall be well, and all manner of thing shall be well.'

In this stark word 'sin' our Lord brought to my mind all things in general that are not good – and the shame, the despising and the utter stripping he accepted for us in this life, and his dying. He also brought to mind all the bodily and spiritual pains and passions of all his creatures.

For we are all stripped in part and shall be, while we follow our master Jesus until we are made pure. That is to say, until we are stripped of our mortal flesh, and of all our inner desires that are not wholly good.

The Cause of Pain is Sin

And all this was shown in a moment and was quickly turned into comfort, for our Lord God does not want the soul to be frightened by this ugly sight. But I did not see sin. For I believe it has no kind of substance or manner of being and that it is only known through the pain it causes. And as for pain, as I see it, it is something temporary, for it cleanses us and makes us know ourselves and ask for forgiveness. And throughout all this the Passion of our Lord comforts us, and it is his blessed will it should do so.

And because of our good Lord's tender love to all those who shall be saved, he quickly comforts them, saying: 'The cause of all this pain is sin. But all shall be well, and all shall be well, and all manner of thing shall be well.' These words were said so kindly and without a hint of blame to me or to any who shall be saved. So how unjust would it be for me to blame God for allowing me to sin, when he does not blame me for falling into it.

And in these words I saw a wonderful high secret hidden in God, and that he will show us this secret openly in heaven. When we know this secret we shall truly see the reason he allowed sin to be, and in the knowledge of this we shall rejoice endlessly in our Lord God.

Cleansing through Suffering

So I saw that Christ has compassion on us because of sin. And just as, before this, I was filled with pain and compassion during Christ's Passion, in the same way I was filled full of compassion for all my fellow-Christians – for those much, much-loved people who shall be saved, that is to say. For God's servants, Holy Church, shall be shaken in sorrow and anguish and tribulation in this world, as a cloth is shaken in the wind. And as to this, our Lord answered in this way: 'I shall make a great occasion out of this in heaven, of endless honour and everlasting joy.'

Yes, I saw so much, that I understood that our Lord, in his pity and compassion, can be pleased by his servants' tribulation. He lays upon every one he longs to bring into his bliss something that is no blame in his sight, but for which they are blamed and despised in this world – scorned, mocked and cast out. He does this to offset the harm they should otherwise have from the pomp and vainglory of this earthly life, and to make their road to him easier, and to bring them higher in his joy without end.

For he says, 'I shall shatter all your vain affections and your vicious pride, and after that I shall gather you up and make you kind and gentle, clean and holy, by joining you to me.'

We Do Not Suffer Alone

And then I saw that every feeling of kinship and compassion that a man feels, in love, for his fellow-Christians, it is Christ within him.

His willingness to be accounted nothing, which was shown in his Passion, was shown over and over again in his compassion – and there are two ways to understand our Lord's meaning in this.

One is the bliss we are brought to, which he wants us to rejoice in. The second is to comfort us in our pain – for it is his will that we should know that our pain shall all be turned to honour and gain by virtue of his Passion, and that we should understand that we do not suffer alone, but with him.

He wills that we should see him as the ground we grow in, and that we see that his pains, and his being counted worthless, go so far beyond anything we can suffer that it cannot be imagined.

Knowing this will save us from grumbling and despair as we suffer our pain. And even if we truly see that we deserve it, yet his love excuses us and in his great courtesy he does away with all our blame. And he upholds us in compassion and pity, as if we were children, innocent and eager.

How Can All Be Well?

But I stayed pondering in grief and sorrow. In my mind I said this to my Lord, in fear and trembling: 'Oh, good Lord, how can all be well when great harm has come to your creatures through sin?' And here I wanted, if I dared, to have some clearer explanation to put my mind at rest.

And to this our blessed Lord answered very gently with a most kind look, and showed that Adam's sin was the worst harm that was done and ever shall be until the world's end. And he also showed that this is clearly known by all Holy Church on earth.

More than this, he taught me that I should look on the glorious Atonement. For this making amends is more pleasing to God and more helpful for the salvation of many, without compare, than ever the sin of Adam was harmful.

What our Lord means by this teaching is that we should remember this: 'Since I have brought good out of the worst-ever evil, I want you to know, by this, that I shall bring good out of all lesser evils, too.'

All Manner of Thing Shall Be Well

One time, our good Lord said: 'All things shall be well.' And another time, he said: 'You shall see for yourself that all manner of thing shall be well.' The soul understood several things from these two sayings.

One was this: that it is his will that we should understand that not only does he take care of great and noble things but also of little and humble things, simple and small – both one and the other. And this is what he means when he says: 'All manner of thing shall be well.' For he wants us to understand that the smallest thing shall not be forgotten.

Something else I understood was this: that we see such evil deeds done, and such great harm caused by them, that it seems to us that it is impossible that any good deed should come out of them. And we look on them, sorrowing and mourning over them, so that we cannot find rest in the joyful sight of God, as we ought to.

The trouble is this – that the range of our thinking is now so blinkered, so little and small, that we cannot see the high, wonderful wisdom and the power and goodness of the blessed Trinity. And this is what he means when he says: 'You shall see for yourself that all manner of thing shall be well.' It was as if he said: 'Have faith, and have trust, and at the last day you shall see it all transformed into great joy.'

A Great Deed To Be Done

There is a Great Deed which the blessed Trinity shall do at the last day, as I see it. And what that deed shall be, and how it shall be done, is unknown to all creatures below Christ. And it shall be hidden until it is done.

He wants us to know of it so that we shall be more at ease in our soul, and at peace in our love, and that we should leave off looking at all the storms that might keep us from the truth, and should rejoice in him.

This is the great deed, ordained by our Lord God since before time began, treasured and hidden in his blessed breast, known only to him, by which he shall make all things well. For just as the blessed Trinity made all things out of nothing, so the same blessed Trinity shall make good all that is not well.

And how it shall be done, there is no creature beneath Christ who knows, nor who shall know until it is done. This is the understanding I had of our Lord's meaning at this time.

The Holding Together of Seeming Opposites

I marvelled greatly at this sight, and looked at our faith, wondering thus: Our faith is grounded in God's word, and a root of our faith is that we believe that God shall keep his word in all things.

And one point of our faith is that many creatures shall be damned, as the angels who fell from heaven through pride are now devils. And men on earth who die out of the faith of Holy Church – that is to say, those who are heathens, and also those who have received the Christian faith but live unchristian lives and so die out of love – all these shall be damned to hell without end, as Holy Church teaches me to believe.

And, understanding all this, I thought it was impossible that all manner of thing should be well, as our Lord showed me at that time. And I had no other answer from our Lord in these showings except this: 'What is impossible for you is not impossible for me. I shall keep my word in all things, and I shall make all things well.'

So I was taught by the grace of God that I should hold steadfastly to the faith, as I had already understood it, and also that I should soberly believe that all things shall be well, as our Lord showed me at that time.

We Shall Be Kept Safe

God brought to my mind that I should sin, and because of the joy I had in looking on him, I was reluctant to look on this Showing. But our Lord was patient with me and gave me grace to listen.

And this showing I took as shown to me personally, but by all the healing comfort that followed, as you shall see, I was taught to see that it was meant for all my fellow-Christians and not just for me. Though our Lord showed me I should sin, by this he meant all, and not just me.

This filled me with quiet fear but our Lord answered: 'I will keep you safe.' These words were said with more love, and certainty, and spiritual consolation than I am allowed or able to tell.

A Godly Will that Never Consents to Sin

For as clearly as I was shown I should sin, just as clearly was the comfort shown – the safekeeping of all my fellow-Christians. What can make me love my fellow-Christians more, than to see that God loves all who shall be saved as if they were one soul?

For in every soul that shall be saved there is a godly will that never agreed to sin, and never shall. Just as there is a beastly will in our lower nature that cannot will any good, so there is a godly will in our higher nature – and this will is so good that it can never will any evil, but only good. And this is why he loves us, and why what we do always pleases him.

By this our Lord showed the whole-hearted love he has for us – yes, that he loves us as much now while we are here on earth as he shall when we stand before his blessed face. And all our troubles come because our own love fails us.

The Sins of the Redeemed Turned to Glory

Also, God showed that sin shall not be a shame to man, but a glory. For just as every sin brings its own suffering, by truth, so every soul that sins earns a blessing by love. And just as many sins are punished with much suffering, because they are so bad, even so they shall be rewarded with many joys in heaven because of the suffering and sorrow they have caused the soul here on earth.

For the soul that comes to heaven is so precious to God, and the place so holy, that God in his goodness never allows a soul that reaches heaven to sin without also seeing that those sins have their reward. And the soul is known to God for ever and joyfully restored with great glory.

In this Showing my understanding was lifted up to heaven. And then God brought happily to my mind David and others without number from the Old Law, and in the New Law he brought to my mind first Mary Magdalene, Peter and Paul, and those of India, and St John of Beverley – and also others without number. And he showed how the Church on earth knows of them and their sins, and it is no shame to them, but is all turned to their glory.

And so our courteous Lord showed them as an example of how it is in part here on earth and shall be fully in heaven. For there, the mark of sin is turned to honour.

The Example of St John of Beverley

As for St John of Beverley, our Lord showed him high in honour to comfort us in our humbleness, and brought to my mind how he is a near neighbour, and well known to us.

And God called him 'St John of Beverley' as plainly as we do, with a glad and happy look, showing that he is a most high saint in God's sight, and a blessed one.

And in this he mentioned that in his youth and early years St John of Beverley was a loyal servant to God, humbly loving and fearing him, and that, nevertheless, God allowed him to fall. But he mercifully upheld him so that he did not perish or lose time.

And afterwards God lifted him up to much more grace. Because of the contrition and humility he had in this life, God has given him many joys in heaven, which go beyond those he would have had if he had not fallen. On earth God shows that this is true by the many miracles that happen continually near his body.

And all this was shown to make us glad and happy in love.

The Scourge of Sin

Sin is the sharpest lash that any chosen soul can be struck with. It is a lash that thrashes men and women and makes them so loathsome in their own sight that for a while they think themselves worthy of nothing but to sink down into hell. But then repentance comes to them by the touch of the Holy Ghost and turns their bitterness to hope for God's mercy. Then he begins to heal their wounds, and the soul begins to wake from death as it turns towards the life of Holy Church.

The Holy Ghost leads the sinner to confession and to acknowledge his sins willingly, openly and truthfully, with great sorrow and with great shame because he has defiled the fair face of God. Then he undertakes a penance for every sin as his confessor lays down. This is a first principle of Holy Church by the teaching of the Holy Ghost.

This is one form of self-abasement which pleases God greatly. Others are bodily illness sent by God; also sorrow and shame that are put upon us, and reproof and the world's contempt – together with all kinds of troubles and temptations we fall into, both bodily and spiritual.

Three Medicines of the Soul

Our Lord holds us tenderly when it seems to us that we are nearly forsaken and cast away because of our sin – and that we deserve to be. And because we are made humble by this we are raised high in God's sight, by his grace, and also by great repentance and compassion and true yearning for God. Then sinners are suddenly delivered from sins and from pain and are taken up to heaven and even made high saints.

Repentance makes us clean; compassion makes us ready; and yearning for God makes us worthy.

These are three ways, as I see it, by which all souls come to heaven – that is to say, those who have been sinners on earth and shall be saved. For by these medicines every soul must be healed.

Shame Shall Be Turned to Honour

Though the soul is healed, God still sees the wounds, and sees them not as scars but as honours. And so, by contrast, as we have been punished here with sorrow and penance, we shall be rewarded in heaven with the courteous love of our Lord God almighty. It is his will that no one who comes there shall lose a whit of his labour, for he looks on sin as sorrow and anguish to those who love him and, because he loves them, does not blame them for it.

The reward we receive shall not be small, but it shall be high, glorious and full of praise; and so shame shall be turned to honour and increase of joy. For our courteous Lord does not want his servants to fall into despair even when we fall deeply into sin, for our falling does not stop him loving us.

Peace and love are always alive in us, but we are not always alive to peace and love. But he wills that we understand this: that he is the ground of our whole life in love, and that he is our ever-lasting protector and mightily defends us against our enemies who fight so hard and fiercely against us. And we need his help all the more because we give them an advantage by our failures.

A Princely Friendship

This is a princely friendship of our courteous Lord, that he looks after us tenderly even while we are in sin. He touches us secretly and shows us our sin by the kindly light of mercy and grace.

When we see ourselves so foul, we believe that God is angry with us because of our sin. Then, through repentance, the Holy Ghost leads us to prayers and to longing with all our hearts to mend our lives, so that God's wrath will be quenched. We do this until such time as we find rest for our soul and ease in our conscience. Then we hope that God has forgiven our sins – and indeed he has.

Then our courteous Lord shows himself to the soul with gladness and delight, with welcoming friendship, as if the soul had been released from pain and prison, saying tenderly: 'My darling, I am glad you have come to me. I have been with you always in all your sorrow, and now you see my love and we are joined in joy.'

Awaiting the Fullness of Joy

And this is how sins are forgiven by mercy and grace and our soul is received in joy – just as it will be when it comes to heaven – whenever this comes about by the gracious working of the Holy Ghost and by virtue of Christ's Passion.

Here I understood truly that all manner of things have been prepared for us by the great goodness of God, and this is so widespread that whenever we are in peace and love we are saved in fact.

But because we may not have this fullness of joy while we are here on earth, we must always strive to live in tender prayer and happy longing towards our Lord Jesus. For he is always longing to bring us to the fullness of joy.

The Danger of Self-Deception

But then, because of all this spiritual comfort that has been promised, a man or a woman might be led, through folly, to say or think: 'If this is true, then it is good to sin so as to get a better reward', or else to think sin less sinful. Beware of this thinking, for truly if this thought comes it is untrue, and comes from the enemy of that true love that shows us all this comfort.

This same blessed love teaches us that we should hate sin simply for the sake of love. And I am sure, by what I feel myself, that the more every loving soul sees of this, in the courteous love of our Lord God, the less he wants to sin and the more he is ashamed.

For if we had to choose between sin and all the pains of hell, and of purgatory, and of earth – death and the rest – when they were not before us, we should choose to bear all those pains rather than sin. For sin is so vile and so greatly to be hated that it can be likened to no other pain – except the pain that is sin.

And I was shown no harder hell than sin, for there is no hell but sin for a loving soul.

We Are to Love the Soul as God Loves It

If we turn our will to love and humbleness, the work of mercy and grace makes us bright and clean. God has as much goodwill towards man, to save him, as he has strength and wisdom.

For Christ himself is the ground of all the laws of Christians, and he taught us to do good to overcome evil. By this we can see that he himself is love, and that he shows us what to do by doing it himself.

For it is his will that we should be like him in wholeness of endless love towards ourselves and our fellow-Christians. And just as he does not stop loving us because of our sin, so he wills that we should not stop loving ourselves or our fellow-Christians – but that we should nakedly hate sin and love the soul for ever, as God loves it. Then we shall hate sin as God hates it, and love the soul as God loves it.

For these words that God spoke are an endless comfort: 'I will keep you safe.'

The Fourteenth Showing

 Prayer makes the soul one with God. For though the soul, restored by grace, is always like God in its nature and substance, it is often unlike God in its condition, because of man's sin.

Then prayer is a witness that the soul's will is the same as God's will and it comforts our conscience and helps us to grace. And so he teaches us to pray, and firmly trust that we shall have what we pray for.

For he looks on us with love and wants to make us his partner in good deeds. And so he leads us to pray for what it is his pleasure to do.

And because we ask him eagerly to do the things he loves to do, it is as if he said: 'What could please me better than to ask me – eagerly, wisely and willingly – to do the very thing I am going to do?'

And so, by prayer, the soul is attuned to God.

In Time of Trouble

When the soul is tempest-tossed, troubled and cut off by worries, then is the time to pray, so as to make the soul willing and responsive towards God. But there is no kind of prayer that can make God more responsive to the soul, for God is always constant in love.

And so I saw that, whenever we feel the need to pray, our good Lord follows us, helping our desire.

And when, by his special grace, we behold him clearly, knowing no other need, then we follow him and he draws us to himself by love.

For I saw and understood that his great overflowing love brings all our gifts to fulfilment.

I saw, too, that his unceasing work in everything is done so well, so wisely and so mightily that it is beyond our power to imagine, or guess, or think.

Two Kinds of Understanding

Now during all this time, from beginning to end, I had two different kinds of understanding.

One was the endless, continuing love, with its assurance of safekeeping and joyful salvation – for this was the message of all the Showings.

The other was the day-to-day teaching of Holy Church, in which I had been taught and grounded beforehand, and which I understood and practised with all my heart. And this was not taken away from me, for I was not turned or led away from it at any point by the Showings. But I was taught, by this, to love it and rejoice in it so that, by the help of our Lord and his grace, I might grow and rise through it to more heavenly knowledge and higher loving.

And so in all these Showings it seemed to me that it was right and proper for us to see and know that we are sinners, and do many evil deeds we ought not to do and leave many good deeds undone that we ought to do, and that we deserve to incur pain and anger because of this.

And, notwithstanding all this, I saw truly that our Lord was never angry, nor never shall be, for he is God.

There Is No Anger in God

He is goodness, life, truth, love and peace. His love and his wholeness cannot allow him to be angry. For I saw truly that it is against the nature of his strength to be angry, and against the nature of his wisdom, and against the nature of his goodness.

God is the goodness that can know no anger, for he is nothing but goodness. Our soul is joined to him – unchangeable goodness – and there is neither anger nor forgiveness between our soul and God, in his sight.

For our soul is wholly joined to God through his own goodness, so there is nothing that can come between God and the soul.

And my soul was led by love and drawn by strength to understand this in every Showing. Our good Lord showed that it is so; and he showed, in truth, that it is so through his great goodness.

And he wills that we should long to understand it – that is, in so far as created things can understand it.

What Is God's Forgiveness and Mercy?

Our soul has a duty to do two things: one is to marvel with awe, and the other is to obey meekly, always rejoicing in God. For it is his will that we know that, in a little while, we shall see plainly in him all that we long for.

And, in spite of all this, I saw and wondered greatly: 'What is the mercy and forgiveness of God?'

For, by the teaching I had beforehand, I understood that the mercy of God should be the forgiveness of his anger which our sin had caused. For I thought the anger of God was worse than any other pain for a soul whose intention and desire is to love.

And so I thought that the forgiveness of his anger should be one of the main points of his mercy.

But in spite of everything that I longed to see – and did see – I could not see this in all the showings.

No Anger except on Man's Part

For I saw no anger, except on man's part, and God forgives this anger in us. For anger is no more than a perversity and striving against peace and love.

And it is caused either by lack of strength, or lack of wisdom, or lack of goodness. This lack is not found in God, but in us.

For we, because of sin and earthliness, have an earthy and continuous striving against peace and love. And he showed that he recognized this many times, by the lovely look of compassion and pity in his face.

For the root of mercy is love, and the work of mercy is our safekeeping in love. And this was shown in such a way that I could not see any part of mercy separately but, as it were, all one love.

Mercy is a sweet, gracious working of love, mingled with pity in plenty. For mercy works and keeps us safe – and mercy works and turns all things to good for us.

The Work of Mercy

Mercy, through love, allows us to fail in some measure. And as much as we fail, so far do we fall. And as far as we fall, by so much do we die.

For we must needs die, so far as we lose the sight and perception of God, who is our life.

Our failing is fearful, our falling is full of shame, and our dying is sorrowful. But in all this, the sweet eye of pity and love never looks away from us, nor does the working of mercy ever cease.

For I saw the property of mercy, and I saw the property of grace, which have two ways of working, in the one love. Mercy has a property of pity like a mother's tender love, and grace has a property of glory, like the royal lordship of love.

Mercy works: it works by safeguarding, by suffering, by giving life and by healing. All this is through the tenderness of love.

The Work of Grace

And grace works: it works by raising up, by rewarding and by always outstripping all that our love and labour deserves. It spreads abroad and shows the high, huge wholeness of God's royal lordship, in his wonderful courtesy. And this is the abundance of love.

For grace turns our fearful failing into overflowing, endless comfort. And grace turns our shameful falling into high, glorious rising. And grace turns our sorrowful dying into holy, blessed life.

For I saw full surely that just as our strivings bring us pain, shame and sorrow here on earth, even so, in contrast, grace brings us comfort, glory and joy in heaven. And it goes so far beyond what we deserve, that when we come up to heaven and receive the sweet reward that grace has given us, then we shall thank and bless our Lord, and rejoice without end that ever we suffered sorrow. And then we shall see a property of blessed love in God which we could never have known if we had not first suffered sorrow.

And when I saw all this, I needs must grant that the purpose of God's mercy and of his forgiveness is to lessen and quench our anger.

God's Anger an Impossibility

For this was a high marvel to the soul, and it was shown continually in all the Showings, and I looked on it carefully: it was shown that, of his nature, our Lord cannot forgive, for he cannot be angry. It would be impossible.

For this was shown: that our life is rooted and grounded in love, and that without love we cannot live. And so to the soul who, by his special grace, sees this much of the high, marvellous goodness of God – and that we are for ever joined to him in love – it is absolutely impossible that God should be angry.

For anger and friendship are two opposites. And so he who quenches and ends our anger must therefore be always loving, gentle and kind – which is the opposite of anger.

For I saw full surely that wherever our Lord appears, peace reigns and anger has no place.

For I saw no whit of anger in God – in short or in long term.

For truly, as I see it, if God could be angry, even a little, we should never have life, or place, or being.

Enfolded in God

For as surely as we owe our being to the endless strength of God, to his endless wisdom and his endless goodness, just as surely we owe our safe-keeping to the endless strength of God, his endless wisdom and his endless goodness.

For though we poor creatures feel debates and strifes within ourselves, yet we are all mercifully enfolded in the gentleness of God, in his kindness, in his benignity, in his goodwill.

For I saw full surely that every good thing – our endless friendship, our dwelling place, our life and our being – are all in God. For the same unending goodness that looks after us while we sin – so we are not cast away – is the same unending goodness that continually makes peace between ourselves and our own anger and strife.

This makes us see the need to beseech God, with true reverence, to forgive us and, through grace, to ask him for salvation. For we cannot be bless-edly saved until we are truly in peace and love. For that is our salvation.

The Safeguarding of God

And though, because of the anger and strivings within us, we are now in trouble, sadness and woe – as befalls those who are blind and who stumble – we are still kept safe and sound by the merciful safeguarding of God, so we are not lost.

But we cannot know the blessed safety or our endless joy until we are filled with peace and love, that is to say, wholly pleased with God and with all his works and with all his judgements, and until we are in love and peace with ourselves and our fellow-Christians and with all that God loves, as love would have it.

And God's goodness in us brings this about.

God Is Our True Peace

So I saw that God is our true peace. He watches over us when we can find no rest, and he works continually to bring us to peace that shall never end.

And when, through the power of mercy and grace, we are made humble and gentle, we are wholly safe. Then suddenly the soul is at one with God, when it is truly at peace with itself, for no anger is found in him.

And so I saw that, when we are full of peace and love, we find no striving in ourselves and are not hindered by the strife that is in us now. For that strife is the cause of our troubles and all our sorrow.

And our Lord takes our strivings and sends them up to heaven where they are made more sweet and delectable than heart can think, or tongue can tell.

And when we get there we shall find them waiting, all turned into lovely and lasting glory.

So God is our sure rock, and he shall be our whole joy, and make us changeless as he is, when we reach heaven.

We Are Not Blamed

And in this mortal life, mercy and forgiveness are the pathway that always leads to grace. And because of the storms and sorrows that befall us we often seem dead, as many judge on earth. But in God's sight the soul that shall be saved is never dead, and never shall be.

But at this I wondered and was amazed with all the strength of my soul and thought this: 'Good Lord, I see that you are truth itself, and I know truly that we sin grievously all the day long and are much to blame. And I can neither forsake knowing this truth, nor do I see you put any blame on us. How can this be?'

For I know by the daily teaching of Holy Church, and by my own feelings, that the blame for our sin hangs heavy upon us, from the first man until the time we come up to heaven.

This, then, was my wonder – that I saw our Lord putting no more blame upon us than if we were as clean and as holy as the angels in heaven.

Julian Herself

Very little is known about Julian. She was born in 1342; and on 8 May 1373, at a time when she and those around her thought she was about to die, she received fifteen visions centred on the Holy Trinity and the Passion of Jesus, and one final vision on the following night. She wrote them down, it seems, soon after receiving them (the Shorter Text), and possibly at about that time dedicated herself to the solitary life, living as an anchoress in a small cell attached to St Julian's Church in Norwich. It is likely that she took her name from the church which would then have been about 400 years old. Her cell, which was pulled down at the Reformation, was rebuilt in 1952 when the church itself was restored after heavy wartime bombing.

Opening out from Julian's cell was a window looking into the church. This enabled her to see Mass being celebrated, and to receive Communion. A second window opposite looked on to the street and from here she would have counselled the many people who must have come to seek her help. In her cell she prayed and meditated upon her visions; later, these were written down, with her reflections on them. No doubt, too, she occupied herself with needlework or some other manual task. At one time or another, two servants – Sara and Alice – attended her bodily needs.

Julian's writings were completed in 1393 and are known today throughout the Christian world as *Revelations of Divine Love*. The work is marked by the depth of its theology, the breadth of its compassion and the almost unrivalled beauty of its language. We know that Julian was still living in 1413 and it may well be that she lived to the age of eighty or beyond. The date of her death is variously conjectured and no trace of her burial place remains. No doubt she is content to have it so. 'You shall soon forget me,' she writes, '(and do so that I shall not hinder you), and behold Jesus who is teacher of all.'

Points of Interest

Enfolded in Love, published by Darton, Longman and Todd, is a simple introduction to Julian's writings drawing on key passages arranged as daily readings.

For the whole text read either Clifton Wolters's Penguin translation entitled *Julian of Norwich*, or *Julian of Norwich – Showings*, published by SPCK and edited by Edmund Colledge and James Walsh. The first book contains the Longer Text only, while the second has both texts.

Who was Julian? by Michael McLean is a good beginner's guide. This pamphlet can be obtained from The Julian Shrine at 75p, post free.

The Julian Shrine lies between Rouen Road and King Street, about half a mile south of Norwich Cathedral. Both St Julian's church and the Lady Julian cell are open every day from dusk to dawn, and regular services are held. Most visitors come desiring to use the church or the cell for private prayer, but a priest or other member of staff is available for many hours each day for any who seek counsel.

A neighbouring guest-house run by Sisters of All Hallows, is available for visitors to the Shrine. Application should be made to the Sister-in-Charge, All Hallows, Rouen Road, Norwich.

The Chaplain may be written to at the same address for particulars of Julian Shrine publications. Requests for prayer should also be sent to him.

The Friends of St Julian's exists to link people by prayer and financial support to the Shrine. The minimum subscription is £1 a year. Application should be made to The Secretary to the Friends of St Julian's, c/o The Rectory, 10 Norman's Buildings, Rouen Road, Norwich.

The Julian Meetings exists to organize and encourage groups to meet regularly for silent contemplative prayer; there are about 150 such groups in the United Kingdom. Particulars can be obtained from Mrs Hilary Burn, Julian Meetings, 5 Geale's Crescent, Alton, Hants GU34 2ND.

Index

The figures in bold type refer to the pages of this book. Those in the second column give the chapters in *Revelations of Divine Love* from which the readings are taken. The third figure indicates which of Julian's sixteen showings is being described.